LIFE IN

DAVID GRAY

SLOW MOTION

WISE PUBLICATIONS
part of The Music Sales Group
London/New York/Paris/Sydney/Copenhagen/Berlin/Madrid/Tokyo

Published by
Wise Publications,
8/9 Frith Street, London, W1D 3JB, England.

Exclusive Distributors:
Music Sales Limited
Distribution Centre, Newmarket Road,
Bury St Edmunds, Suffolk, IP33 3YB, England.

Music Sales Pty Limited
120 Rothschild Avenue, Rosebery,
NSW 2018, Australia.

Order No. AM983741
ISBN 1-84609-238-8
This book © Copyright 2005 by Wise Publications,
a division of Music Sales Limited.

Original CD design by Farrow Design.
Music arranged by Derek Jones.
Music processed by Paul Ewers Music Design.

Printed & bound in the United Kingdom.

www.musicsales.com

ALIBI

Words & Music by David Gray

Stone blind a - li - bi, I will eat the lie,_____ find the word. Could break_____ a - ny spell that binds you.

Prayers like am - mon - ites curl be - neath the lights,_____ how I long to bite_____ ev'ry hand that feeds you

11

THE ONE I LOVE

Words & Music by David Gray & Craig McClune

tra - cer glides___   in it's grace-ful arc,___
might have said,___   on - ly wish I could,___

send a lit - tle prayer___ out to___ ya_____ 'cross the
now I'm leak-ing life_____ fast - er_____ than I'm

fall - ing dark.___ } Tell the re - po___ man
leak - ing blood.___ }

and the stars a - bove___   you're the

13

one I love.____ Yeah.____

2. Per-fect You're the one I love.____

The one I love.__ Yeah.____

LATELY

Words & Music by David Gray, Craig McClune,
Robert Malone, Tim Bradshaw & David Nolte

time well spent,_ on a time that_ ain't____ no more._ Taste the

bro - ken hearts_ in the va - cant lots,_ see the fruit that rots_____ on the
(2.) salt - ed kiss_ from this cup of bliss,_ watch a new lie twist_____ on the

trees._____ Try to turn my head, leave it all for dead,_ but it's
breeze._____ You can paint it red, leave it all for dead,_ but it's

in my_ mind___ al - ways._ Ho - ney, late - ly I've been
in my_ head___ al - ways._

I could have said in ad - vance. You saw it all at a glance___ and good - bye.___

Good - bye.___

1.

2. Drag a

2.

Good - bye.___

Good - bye.___

Ho - ney,

21

late - ly,   ho - ney,   late - ly   I've been

1.

way   down._   Ho - ney, late - ly_____   I've been way   down._   Ho - ney,

2.

way   down._   Late - ly._____

rit.

Late - ly._____

22

NOS DA CARIAD

Words & Music by David Gray, Craig McClune,
Robert Malone, Tim Bradshaw & David Nolte

27

SLOW MOTION

Words & Music by David Gray & Craig McClune

1. While I was watch-ing you did a slow dis- solve,___ while I was watch-ing
4. Snow-flakes are fall-ing, I'll catch them in my hand.___ Snow-flakes are fall-ing,

FROM HERE YOU CAN ALMOST SEE THE SEA

Words & Music by David Gray

1. Come the week-end__ and we'll be long gone,__
(2.) hold still,__ could make a clean in -
(3.) high clouds__ flushed with the light of__

see____ the sea.____

1. ... **2.**

2. If you would

Bm

Just a-no-ther fool in the line.____

A

Ah.____

E

D.S. al Coda

3. I dream of

Fin - gers, knees and knuck - les scraped,__ all of the rub - bish heaped,__ __ a piece of card-board taped__ up where the bed-room win - dow pane__ used to be. From here you can al - most,__ from here you can al - most see__

I saw a film once__ where all the air - holes__ froze up.__ A kill - er whale swam__ un - der the blue ice____ till her heart stopped.

AIN'T NO LOVE

Words & Music by David Gray

1. May - be that it would do me good___ if I be - lieved___ there were a God___
2. Some - days I'm burst - ing at the seams___ with all my half___ re - mem - bered dreams___

___ out in the star - ry fir - ma - ment. But as it is it's just a
___ and then it shoots me down a - gain. I feel the damp - ness as it

lie and I'm here eat - ing up the bore - dom on an is - land of ce -
creeps, I hear you cough - ing in your sleep___ be - neath a bro - ken win - dow -

- ment. Give me your ec - sta - cy, I'll feel it, op - en win - dow and I'll
-pane. To - mor - row, girl, I'll buy you chips, a lol - li - pop to stain your

-ches like a thou - sand dia - mond buds. Wait - ing there in ev - 'ry pause,

____ that old fa - mil - iar fear that claws____ you, tells you no - thing ain't no

good. Then pull - ing back, you see it all,____ down here so laugh - a - ble and small,

____ hard - ly a quiv - er in the dirt. This ain't no love that's guid - ing me.

44

HOSPITAL FOOD

Words & Music by David Gray & Robert Malone

1. Just a lit-tle some-thing for the pain.
2. So patch me up boys, take me home.
3. Don't seem to have that much to show,

Tell me some - thing,___ tell me some-

thing___ I don't_____ al - rea___ - dy___ know.

Tell me some - thing,___ tell me some - thing I___ don't know.___

D.S. al Coda

Coda I

Ah,___ you've stood in the roar,___ you've tast - ed

the snow.___ Tell me some - thing,___

tell me some - thing___ I don't_____ al - rea-

- dy___ know.___ Tell me some - thing,___ tell me some-

NOW AND ALWAYS

Words & Music by David Gray

cont. sim.

1. You're in my mind,___ ba - by, now and___ al - ways.
2. A bon - fire smok - ing in - to a low sky.

You're in my mind,___ ba - by, now and___
The sparks they fly___ up in - to a

___ al - ways.___
low sky.___

The road I'm walk -
Would that these de -

- ing might fall a - way.___
- mons would let me rest.___

You're in my mind,___ ba - by, now and___ al - ways.
They're with me, Lord,___ till the day that___ I___ die.

Am
D

Feast my eyes on___

Em
C

___ sa - cred___ lies.___

%. G

2. Ill wind that blows___ in from all___ di - rec - tions.
3. You're in my mind,___ ba - by, now and___ al - ways.___
4. The swans like ghosts___ on the jet black___ wa - ter.

for your own_____ pro - tec - tion.
ba - by, now and____ al - ways.
on the star - ry____ wa - ter.____

Am D Em C

Feast my eyes on_____ sa - cred_____ lies.__

F

D♭

57

58

DISAPPEARING WORLD

Words & Music by David Gray

1. Slow-ly the truth is load-ing. I'm weight-ed down with love.
2. We're thread-ing hope like fire, down through the des-perate blood.

Snow ly-ing deep and ev-en.
Down through the trail-ing wire,

Strung out and dream-ing of...
in - to the leaf - less wood.

Night fall-ing on the ci-

- ty,

quite some - thing to be-hold.

Don't it just look so pret-ty, this dis-ap-pear - ing

1.
world.

2.
world,

61

this dis-ap-pear - ing___ world.___

I'll be stick-ing right___ there with___ it, I'll be by your side.__

(Na na na na na na.) Sail-ing like a sil - ver bull - et, hit 'em

'tween the eyes.__ (Na na na na na na.) Through the smoke and ris -

2 3 4 5 6 7 8 9
10/05(56536)